First World War
and Army of Occupation
War Diary
France, Belgium and Germany

14 DIVISION
42 Infantry Brigade
Manchester Regiment
16th Battalion
4 July 1918 - 6 June 1919

WO95/1900/3

The Naval & Military Press Ltd
www.nmarchive.com
Published in association with The National Archives

Published by

The Naval & Military Press Ltd

Unit 10 Ridgewood Industrial Park,

Uckfield, East Sussex,

TN22 5QE England

Tel: +44 (0) 1825 749494

www.naval-military-press.com

www.nmarchive.com

This diary has been reprinted in facsimile from the original. Any imperfections are inevitably reproduced and the quality may fall short of modern type and cartographic standards.

© Crown Copyright
Images reproduced by permission of The National Archives, London, England, 2015.

Contents

Document type	Place/Title	Date From	Date To
Heading	WO95/1900/3 14 Division 42 Infantry Brigade July 1918-Jun 1919 16th Battalion Manchester Reg		
Heading	14th Division 42nd Infy Bde 16th Bn Manchr Regt Jly 1918-Jun 1919		
Heading	War Diary Of 16th Manchester Regt From 1.7.18 To 31.7.18 Volume No. 33		
War Diary	Folkestone	04/07/1918	04/07/1918
War Diary	Boulogne	04/07/1918	04/07/1918
War Diary	Baincthun	05/07/1918	05/07/1918
War Diary	Mesnil	11/07/1918	11/07/1918
War Diary	Sanghen	12/07/1918	12/07/1918
War Diary	Tournehem	13/07/1918	17/07/1918
Heading	War Diary Secret 16th Manchester Regt. August 1918 From 1-8-18 To 31-8-18 Vol 34		
War Diary	Tournehem	05/08/1918	17/08/1918
War Diary	Tunnelling Camp	23/08/1918	23/08/1918
War Diary	Arrival Camp	29/08/1918	29/08/1918
Heading	War Diary Of 16th Manchester Regt From 1-9-18 To 30-9-18 Volume No 35		
War Diary	Arrival Farm (Ypres Sector)	29/08/1918	05/09/1918
War Diary	Ypres Sector.	05/09/1918	10/09/1918
War Diary	Brake Camp	13/09/1918	14/09/1918
War Diary	Winnezeele	15/09/1918	15/09/1918
War Diary	Dominion Camp	19/09/1918	19/09/1918
War Diary	Dickebusch Bund.	20/09/1918	21/09/1918
War Diary	Voormezeele	21/09/1918	22/09/1918
War Diary	Ouderdom	26/09/1918	27/09/1918
War Diary	Elzenwalle	27/09/1918	28/09/1918
War Diary	Micmac Camp	29/09/1918	29/09/1918
Heading	16th Battalion Manchester Regiment. War Diary Appendix 1 Casualty List		
Heading	Volume XXXVI 16th Battalion Manchester Regiment. War Diary For The Month Of October 1918		
War Diary	Micmac	01/10/1918	01/10/1918
War Diary	Neuve Eglise	02/10/1918	02/10/1918
War Diary	Hell-Fire Corner.	03/10/1918	03/10/1918
War Diary	Zonnebeke	04/10/1918	12/10/1918
War Diary	Dranoutre-Kemmel	13/10/1918	14/10/1918
War Diary	Wulverghem	15/10/1918	15/10/1918
War Diary	Comines	16/10/1918	17/10/1918
War Diary	La Barbe	18/12/1918	19/12/1918
War Diary	Luingne	20/10/1918	20/10/1918
War Diary	Espierres	21/10/1918	23/10/1918
War Diary	Dottignies	24/10/1918	28/10/1918
War Diary	Front Line Espierres	29/10/1918	31/10/1918
Miscellaneous	16th Battalion Manchester Regiment. War Diary For October 1918 Appendix I	31/10/1918	31/10/1918
Miscellaneous	16th Battalion Manchester Regiment. War Diary For October 1918 Honours & Awards. Military Medal B51516 Private Poolton H.	31/10/1918	31/10/1918

Heading	16th Bn Manchester Regiment. War Diary November 1918 Volume 37		
War Diary	Espierres	31/10/1918	01/11/1918
War Diary	Les Balons	01/11/1918	08/11/1918
War Diary	Petit Audenarde	08/11/1918	13/11/1918
War Diary	Les Ballon	14/11/1918	30/11/1918
Heading	16th Bn Manchester Regiment. War Diary November 1918 Casualties Nil. Appendix 1		
Heading	16th Bn Manchester Regiment. Appendix 2. War Diary. November 1918 Honours & Awards. In November 1918 Appendix 2		
Heading	16th Battalion Manchester Regiment War Diary December 1918 Volume 38		
War Diary	Les Balons	01/12/1918	31/12/1918
Miscellaneous	16th Bn Manchester Regiment. Appendix 1.		
Heading	16th B Manchester Regiment. War Diary For January 1919 Volume 39		
War Diary	Les Balons Herseau	01/01/1919	31/01/1919
Miscellaneous	16th B Manchester Regiment Appendix 1.		
Heading	16th Bn Manchester Regiment War Diary February 1919		
War Diary	Les Balons Herseaux Belgium	01/02/1919	28/02/1919
Heading	16th B Manchester Regiment. War Diary For March 1919 Volume 41.		
War Diary	Les Balons	13/01/1919	31/01/1919
Heading	16th Battalion Manchester Regiment. War Diary April 1919 Volume 42		
War Diary	Les Ballons Herseaux Belgium	01/04/1919	30/04/1919
War Diary	Les Ballons Herseaux Belgium	01/05/1919	31/05/1919
War Diary	Les Ballons	01/06/1919	06/06/1919

WO 95   1900/3

14 Division
42 Infantry Brigade

July 1918 – Jan 1919.

16th Battalion
Manchester Reg

14TH DIVISION
42ND INFY BDE

16TH BN MANCHR REGT

JLY 1918-JUN 1919

*From 30 Div.
90 Bde*

C O N F I D E N T I A L

W A R   D I A R Y

OF

16ᵀᴴ MANCHESTER REGT

FROM 1-7-18 TO 31-7-18

VOLUME NO. 33

Army Form C. 2118

WAR DIARY
or
INTELLIGENCE SUMMARY.

(Erase heading not required.)

Instructions regarding War Diaries and Intelligence Summaries are contained in F. S. Regs., Part II. and the Staff Manual respectively. Title pages will be prepared in manuscript.

Place	Date	Hour	Summary of Events and Information	Remarks and references to Appendices
FOLKESTONE	4.7.18		The Battn entrained at Brookwood at 11.45 p.m (3/7/18) and 12.15 a.m. (4/7/18) arriving FOLKESTONE at 3.15 a.m. and 3.45 a.m. Embarked at 9 a.m.	
BOULOGNE	4.7.18		The Battn disembarked at BOULOGNE and marched to OSTROHOVE REST CAMP	
BAINCTHUN	5.7.18		The Battn marched to BAINCTHUN	
MESNIL	11.7.18		The Battn marched to MESNIL	
SANGHEN	12.7.18		The Battn marched to SANGHEN	
TOURNEHEM	13.7.18		The Battn marched to TOURNEHEM	
"	17.7.18	2.30 p.m	The Battn was inspected by General Sir Herbert C.O. Plumer G.C.B., G.C.M.G., G.C.V.O., A.D.C., Commanding Second Army.	
"	"	8.0 p.m	A draft of 394 O.R. joined the Battn from garrison Battns Base Depot. (Category B1.) From 14th to 31st July the Battn was employed in general training	
			Casualties during month :- NIL	
			Honours and Awards :- NIL	

Kindler
for. LIEUT COLONEL
MAJOR
Commanding 18th

WAR DIARY

42/14

SECRET

16TH MANCHESTER REGT.
August 1918.

FROM 1-8-18   TO 31-8-18

VOL 34

WAR DIARY
INTELLIGENCE SUMMARY
(Erase heading not required.)

Army Form C. 2118.

Place	Date	Hour	Summary of Events and Information	Remarks and references to Appendices
TOURNEHEM	5/8/18		14th Divisional Horse Shows were held at EPERLECQUES. The Battalion won first prize for Best Cooker and Pair and second prize in the Open Event for Best Cooker & Pair.	
	17/8/18		Battalion Sports were held in the Cricket Field, GUEMY.	
	23/8/18		Battalion marched from TOURNEHEM to NORTKERQUE and entrained 18th Bn. Detrained at PROVEN and marched to TUNNELLING CAMP. (Sheet 27. L.4.d.)	
TUNNELLING CAMP.				
ARRIVAL CAMP	24/8/18		Battalion proceeded by Light Railway to ARRIVAL CAMP (Sheet 28 - B.28.) A.C.3. relieving 1/5th K.O.S.B.s in the Left Divisional Sector of the II Corps Front. The 42nd Inf. Bde. became Brigade in Reserve. From Aug 1st to Aug 22nd the Bn. were engaged in Training at TOURNEHEM.	
			Casualties : NIL. Honours & Awards : NIL.	

W.H. Bottley
Lt. Col. Comdg.
16th Manchester Regt.

31-8-18.

CONFIDENTIAL

WAR DIARY

OF

16th MANCHESTER REGT

FROM 1-9-18 TO 30-9-18

VOLUME NO
35

Army Form C. 2118.

WAR DIARY
or
INTELLIGENCE SUMMARY.
(Erase heading not required.)

Instructions regarding War Diaries and Intelligence Summaries are contained in F. S. Regs., Part II. and the Staff Manual respectively. Title pages will be prepared in manuscript.

Place	Date	Hour	Summary of Events and Information	Remarks and references to Appendices
	1918			
ARRIVAL FARM (YPRES SECTOR)	Aug 29th to Sept. 5th.		In Support YPRES SECTOR. The Battalion Band rejoined the Battalion at Details, BRAKE CAMP Sept. 3rd. 1918. from 'R' Depot.	
YPRES SECTOR.	5th 6th 9th.		The Bn relieved the 23rd Bn London Rifle Brigade Regt. in the line on the right of the left Sub-sector-YPRES SECTOR. B & C Coys in the Front Line ; A Coy in Support ; D Coy in Reserve ; Bn H.Q. in RAMPARTS, YPRES.	
	9/10th.		A & D Coys relieved C & B Coys in the Front Line.	
BRAKE CAMP	13/14th.		The Bn was relieved in the Front Line by 29th D.L.I. On relief the Bn marched to BRAKE CAMP. 28.A.24.b.	
WINNEZEELE	15th.		The Bn entrained and proceeded by Light Railway to WINNEZEELE where they were billetted in an area between that place and STEENWOORDE.	
DOMINION CAMP.	19th.		The Bn proceeded by Bus to DOMINION CAMP 28/ G.23.b. The Transport moved by road.	
DICKEBUSCH BUND.	20/21st.		The Bn moved by march route to DICKEBUSCH AREA.	
VOORMEZEELE	21/22nd		The Bn relieved the 14th Bn A. & S. H. in the Bde Sector VOORMEZEELE. A & B Coys in Front line ; C Coy in Support ; D Coy in Reserve in SCOTTISH WOOD.	
OUDERDOM.	26/27th.		The Bn was relieved in the line by 6th Bn Wilts Regt and 14th Bn A. & S. H. On relief Bn H.Q., A, B & D Coys marched to OUDERDOM. C Coy marched to DICKEBUSCH BUND.	

Sheet 2. (continued).

Army Form C. 2118.

WAR DIARY
or
INTELLIGENCE SUMMARY.

(Erase heading not required.)

Instructions regarding War Diaries and Intelligence Summaries are contained in F. S. Regs., Part II. and the Staff Manual respectively. Title pages will be prepared in manuscript.

Place	Date	Hour	Summary of Events and Information	Remarks and references to Appendices
ELZENWALLE.	27/28th.		The Bn, less C Coy, marched to ELZENWALLE AREA. 28/H.36.c. and became Battalion in Support. C Coy remained in DICKEBUSCH HUTS.	
	28th.	5.30 a.m.	at 5.30 a.m. the Brigade attacked and gained all their objectives, the support Bn not being called on to take any active part. C Coy carried S.A.A. and Stores from HEMEL DUMP to the front line after the objectives had been gained.	
MICMAC CAMP.	29th.		The Bn marched to MICMAC CAMP 28/H.31.b. The Bde was not formally relieved. The two Divisions on the flanks having joined hands in front of the line held by the Division.	
			Honours and Awards. NIL.	Appendix.1.
			Casualties: Officers. Wounded in Action. 1.	See Casualties.
			Other Ranks. Killed. 4. Wounded. 23. Missing. NIL.	

W H Colley Lt. Col Commdg.,
16th Battalion Manchester Regiment

16th Battalion Manchester Regiment.

WAR DIARY.

APPENDIX 1. Casualty List.

2/Lt E.C.P.Dewing, W in A. 25.9.18.

B77115 Pte Dunn A. K in A. 28.9.18.
A303010 " Davies. -do- 26.9.18.
A64401 " Dilworth A. -do- 25.9.18.
B64516 Pte Mulvaney H. -do- 22.9.18.

A250626 Pte Edwards W. W in A 21.9.18.
A204001 Pte Keeling J. -do- 22.9.18.
A64436 Pte Stevens L.G. -do- 21.9.18.
B3812 L/Sgt Bradbury G. -do- 22.9.181
B64534 Pte Hough H. -do- 22.9.18.
B51145 Pte Wood G.J. -do- 23.9.18.
C77102 Pte Bestwick -do- 26.9.18.
A61515 Pte Cooks L. -do- 26.9.19.
A252668 Pte Dowd W. -do- "
B77684 Pte Coupe S. -do- "
B6325 B.S.M. Williams S.R.-do- "
B64459 Pte Bush A J. -do- "
A352688 Pte Lomas J. -do- "
A77370 " Hogan P. -do- 27.9.18.
A61514 Pte Cave W. -do- 24.9.18.
A77126 Pte Gregory A. -do- 27.9.18.
B77666 Pte Wright W.H. -do- 27.9.18.
B77140 Pte Plumbe W. -do- 28.9.18.
B252936 Pte Ley F.J. -do- 27.9.18.
B77149 Pte Ward H. -do- 26.9.18.
A64438 Pte Tunnell W.H. -do- 26.9.18.
B252994 Pte Willmott F.H.-do- 26.9.18.
C64604 Pte Lloyd W.J. -do- 28.9.19.

VOLUME XXXVI.

16TH BATTALION MANCHESTER REGIMENT.

WAR DIARY

FOR THE MONTH OF

OCTOBER 1918.

In the Field.   Mershaw. Major, Commanding,
31.10.1918.   16th Battalion Manchester Regiment.

SHEET 1.

WAR DIARY
or
INTELLIGENCE SUMMARY.

(Erase heading not required.)

Army Form C. 2118.

Instructions regarding War Diaries and Intelligence Summaries are contained in F. S. Regs., Part II. and the Staff Manual respectively. Title pages will be prepared in manuscript.

Place	Date	Hour	Summary of Events and Information	Remarks and references to Appendices
Micmac	1918. Oct.1st	12.30.	The Batt. marched from Micmac Camp to WYTCHAETE area 28 S W. C14.15.25. Battalion H.Q in Pill Box.	
NEUVE EGLISE.	2nd.	11.00.	Bn marched to NEUVE EGLISE via WULVERGHEM. On arrival stopped for two hours by roadside near DAYLIGHT CORNER. Orders being issued from Bde to entrain on Light Railway at T.4.d at 18.15 hours to HELL FIRE JUNCTION,YPRES. Stores and Rations being taken to that place by Lorries. Transport moved next day after picking up other stores from Dump.	
HELL-Fire Corner.	3rd.		Bn spent the day in Old Front Line White Chateau, resting in shelters and Dug outs.	
ZONNEBEKE.	4th.	16.30.	Bn entrained at HELL-FIRE Junction,Light Rly,and proceeded to ZONNEBEKE detraining at ALMA 28 N.E./ D22.a.3.3. Billets in Old Dug outs shelters & Tents. Transport Lines moved to ROME FARM VLAMERTINGHE.	
ZONNEBEKE.	5/12th		Battalion engaged as Working Party on roads,earning high praise from Corps on work accomplished.	
DRANOUTRE-KEMMEL.	13th.	06.30.	Bn marched to HELL-FIRE junction and entrained for DRANOUTRE-KEMMEL Area detraining at PADDINGTON junction Billeted in Dug Outs,shelters etc at 28 S.W.N31.c.	
do.	14th.		Bn rested and awaited Orders . Baths. Vicinity of Camp shelled with High Velocity Guns. No Casualties.	
WULVERGHEM.	15th.	09.00.	Bn moved to WULVERGHEM and rested in Tents awaiting Orders Transport & Stores also moved with Bn . At 17.30 hrs orders were received to Mbus at WULVERGHEM Cross Rds . Debussed at MAI.CORNET V.3.a.0.9. and took up position in front of COMINES. Transport Lines remained at WULVERGHEM.	

WAR DIARY or INTELLIGENCE SUMMARY.

SHEET 2.

Army Form C. 2118.

(Erase heading not required.)

Place	Date	Hour	Summary of Events and Information	Remarks and references to Appendices
COMINES.	1918 Oct. 16th.		The Battalion occupied Posts in front of COMINES.	
	17th.		The Battalion under verbal orders marched to LA BARRE transport & Stores followed up and rested the night there.	
LA BARRE.	18th.	11.00.	Battalion with transport marched to BETHLEEM NEUVILLE EN-FERRAIN area 28. S.E/ being Billeted the night in houses.	
do.	19th	08.40.	Bn with Transport marched to MONTREUX area being billeted in Houses awaiting orders. At 16.15 hrs the Bn marched to LUINGNE to Billets.	
LUINGNE	20th	09.00	Bn with transport marched to QUEVACAMPS area 9799/9800 B.3.d. Enemy rearguard fighting in next village. The Battalion being billeted in houses.	
ESPIERRES	21.		The Bn moved to front line at ESPIERRES A. Coy in reserve B Coy in support C Coy on road C.D.d. D Coy 0.9.a.	
do.	23.	night of.	Bn relieved by 6th Wilts and proceeded to BOTTIGNES where billeted	
BOTTIGNES	24/27.		Bn engaged in cleaning up and refitting. Training carried out. Town shelled occasionally.	
do.	27/28.	night of.	Bn relieved half the 6th Wilts and one Coy of the 2/17 London Regiment in the Line on night of 27/28. 14th A.& S.Hldrs on left and a Bn of the 121 Bde on right. A Coy relieved B Coy 2/17th London Regt. BCoy relieved C Coy of the 6th Wilts, D Coy relieved B Coy of the 6th Wilts. "C" Coy in chateau at C.2.d.8.5.	

Army Form C.2118.

WAR DIARY
or
INTELLIGENCE SUMMARY.
(Erase heading not required.)

Sheet 3.

Instructions regarding War Diaries and Intelligence Summaries are contained in F. S. Regs., Part II. and the Staff Manual respectively. Title pages will be prepared in manuscript.

Place	Date	Hour	Summary of Events and Information	Remarks and references to Appendices
Front Line ESPIERRES.	Oct. 29/30.	22.00 hrs	On the night of 29/30 Oct Two Platoons of "A" Coy and Two Platoons of "B" Coy sucessfully carried out a Minor Operation, crossing the River SCHELT at Two places and establishing Posts on the East Bank. Five unwounded prisoners and Two Machine Guns were captured. The Bn congratulated on sucess by G.O.C. Division.	Appendix 1 Casualties. Appendix 2 Honours & Awards.
	31/1st.		The Battalion was relieved by the 18th Bn Yorks & Lancs Rest and marched to Transport Lines (relief completed 23.48 hrs). Bn rested at Transport Lines and after breakfast had been served marched to Billets near WATTRELOS sheet 29 & 37/A.15.b.0.8.	
			Casualties. Appendix 1.	
			Other Ranks : Killed 7. D of W. 1. Wounded 12.	
			Honours & Awards. Appendix 2.	

[signature] Major, Commanding
16th Battalion Manchester Regiment.

16TH BATTALION MANCHESTER REGIMENT.

WAR DIARY FOR OCTOBER 1918.

APPENDIX 1.

Casualties.

Killed in Action.

B64523	Pte Fallon T.	11.10.18.
D64507	Pte Stanton H.	22.10.18.
B77439	L/C Dawson F.T.	29.10.18.
B61586	Pte Carman P.	-do-
A64405	Pte Bourke H.	-do-
D252920	Pte Dymond C.H.	-do-
C252946	Pte Eckersall T.	-do-

Died of Wounds.

C64579	Pte Mason D.	29.10.18.

Wounded in Action.

B64525	Pte	Humphreys H.	29.10.18.
D64466	"	Hammond J.	-do-
C201400	"	Shaw E.	30.10.18.
A350438	"	Lewis JR.	-do-
C64585	"	Shephard W.H.	-do-
A245820	L/C	Lund N.	-do-
B77456	Pte	Broomfield H.	-do-
C64557	"	Parker WO.	-do-
B64524	Pte	Fox G.	11.10.18.
B64496	"	Nelson RW.	11.10.18.
D59689	"	Davies G.	22.10.18.
D64439	L/C	Plume H.	23.10.18.

31.10.18.

Major, Commanding,
16th Battalion Manchester Regiment.

16th BATTALION MANCHESTER REGIMENT.

WAR DIARY FOR OCTOBER 1918.

HONOURS & AWARDS.

MILITARY MEDAL.

B51516 Private POOLTON H.

31.10.18.

Major, Commanding,
16th Battalion Manchester Regiment.

16th Bn Manchester Regiment.
....

WAR DIARY.

November 1918.

VOLUME 37.

....

In the Field.
30.11.18.

..W.H.Colley....LIEUT-COLONEL.
COMMANDING 16TH BN MANCHESTER REGIMENT.

Army Form C. 2118.

WAR DIARY
or
INTELLIGENCE SUMMARY.
(Erase heading not required.)

Instructions regarding War Diaries and Intelligence Summaries are contained in F.S. Regs., Part II. and the Staff Manual respectively. Title pages will be prepared in manuscript.

Place	Date	Hour	Summary of Events and Information	Remarks and references to Appendices
ESPIERRES	31.10.18 to 1.11.18.		On the night of Oct.31st/Nov.1st the Battalion was relieved by the 18th Yorks & Lancs and proceeded to Transport lines where Bn rested and at 0600 hrs after a hot breakfast, marched to Billets at LES BALONS- WATTRELOS.	
Les BALONS.	1/11/18 to 8/11/18.		Battalion engaged in Cleaning up, resting, refitting and training.	
PETIT AUDENARDE	8/11/18.	15.15.	Battalion moved by march route to PETIT AUDENARDE, resting the night there.	
	9/11/18	11.00	Following Brigade telephone message, the Battalion marched to DOTTIGNIES occupying Billets. Q.M. stores also billeted in Town. Transport in farm on outskirts of town.	
	9/11/18 to 11/11/18		The Battalion stood by awaiting pending operations.	
	11.11.18.		Message received at 10.20 from G.H.Q. via Brigade that Hostilities cease at 11.00 hrs November 11th.1918.	
	11.11.18. to 13.11.18.		Battalion rested at DOTTIGNIES.	
LES BALLON.	14.11.18.		Battalion moved by march route to LES BALLON - WATTRELOS.	
	14.11.18. to 30.11.18.		Battalion engaged in smartening up, ceremonial parades, and sent a detachment to help Farmers in Agricultural Work. Sports and Pastimes generally indulged in.	

Appendix 1. Casualties- Nil.
Appendix 2. Honours & Awards.

W.H.Bolley
Lieut-Col.Commdg.,
16th Battalion Manchester Regt.

16th Bn Manchester Regiment.   Appendix 1.

WAR   DIARY.   NOVEMBER.1918.

CASUALTIES.

N I L .

In the Field.   W H Colley......Lieut-Col.
30.11.18.   Commanding 16th Bn Manchester Regiment.

16th Bn Manchester Regiment.

Appendix. 2.

WAR DIARY. NOVEMBER. 1918.

Honours & Awards, in November. 1918.

2/Lieut. R COMPTON.   Military Cross.
                      Auth: D.R.O. 207 dated 13.11.18.

In the Field.
30.11.18.   W H Colley........Lieut-Col.
                         Commanding 16th Bn Manchester Regt.

16th Battalion MANCHESTER REGIMENT.

WAR DIARY. December 1918.

VOLUME 38.

In the Field.
31.12.18.

W. H. Bolley Lieut-Colonel.
Commanding 16th Bn Manchester Regiment.

WAR DIARY or INTELLIGENCE SUMMARY.

Army Form C. 2118.

Place	Date	Hour	Summary of Events and Information	Remarks and references to Appendices
Les BAIONS.	1.12.18 to 31.12.18.		During the month of December the Battalion remained in Billets at Les BAIONS? HERSEAUX. BELGIUM Battalion parades in mornings and recreational Training engaged in.	
			Casualties - NIL Honours and awards. Appendix 1.	

Appendix.1.

16th Bn Manchester Regiment.

Honours and awards   War Diary. Dec 1918.

MILITARY CROSS.

2/Lieutenant F SOUTHWORTH.

Military Medal.

57326. Sergeant J. E. EBLING.

Mentioned in SIR D.HAIG's Despatches. L.G.Supp. dated 28.12.18

Lieut-Colonel W.ELSTOB.D.S.O. M.C.   (Killed in Action 21.3.18)
A/Capt. A.C.ABBA. M.M.
R.S.M. H. Kelly.

      W. H. Colley Lieut-Colonel.
     Commanding 16th Bn Manchester Regiment.

16th B Manchester Regiment.

WAR DIARY.

for January. 1919. Volume. 39.

I the Field.
31.1.19.

W. H. Colley..........Lieut-Colonel.
Commanding 16th BN Manchester Regiment.

WAR DIARY
or
INTELLIGENCE SUMMARY.
(Erase heading not required.)

Army Form C. 2118.

Place	Date	Hour	Summary of Events and Information	Remarks and references to Appendices
LES BRLONS.	1919 Jan 1.		The Battalion remained in Billets. Recreational Training.	
HERSEAU.	Jan 16		Lecture. Sports. Educational Classes held.	
	Jan 31		Demobilization of Officers & men proceeded with. A Colour Party consisting of Capt T. Jenkins M.C.,D.C.M. M.M. and 2/Lt G.S. Knipf, two Warrant Officers, 6 Sgts and 32 Rank & File proceeded to the Square ROUBAIX, Jan 25th 1919 for the presentation of the Battalion Colours by Lieut-General Sir Beauvoir De Lisle K.C.B.D.S.O Commanding fifth Army.	
			Casualties. Nil. Honours & Awards. Appendix 1	

W.H.E. Utley
Commanding 1/6th Loyal N. Lancashire

16th B. Manchester Regiment.   Appendix.1.

Honours And Awards. Jan 1919.

Meritorious Service Medal.

6694. C.Q.M.S. TYLDESLEY. A.J.

Auth: L.G.Supp. dated 18.1.19.

In the Field.
31.1.19.
          W.H.Colley........Lieut-Colonel.
          Commanding 16th Bn. Manchester Regt.

16th BN MANCHESTER REGIMENT.

WAR DIARY.

FEBRUARY.1919.

Les Balo s.
Herseaux.

................Major.
Comma di g 16th B Ma chester Regt.

WAR DIARY
or
INTELLIGENCE SUMMARY
(Erase heading not required.)

Army Form C. 2118.

Place	Date	Hour	Summary of Events and Information	Remarks and references to Appendices
LES BALONS	1/2/19	6	The Battalion remained in billets at LES BALONS, and were rapidly demobilised. Two companies were formed on 4th Feby. Total ration strength on 28th Feby 289.	
HERSEAUX Belgium	28/2/19		Known Rewards - Nil. Casualties - Nil.	Martin Major

16th B. Manchester Regiment.

WAR DIARY.
FOR
MARCH 1919.

VOLUME 41.

Les Balons
HERSEAUX.

31.3.19.

W.H. Colley.....Lieut-Colonel.
Commanding 16th Bn Manchester Regiment.

Army Form C 2118.

WAR DIARY
or
INTELLIGENCE SUMMARY.
(Erase heading not required.)

Instructions regarding War Diaries and Intelligence Summaries are contained in F. S. Regs., Part II. and the Staff Manual respectively. Title pages will be prepared in manuscript.

Place	Date	Hour	Summary of Events and Information	Remarks and references to Appendices
Les Balons.	13.1.19 to 31.1.19.		The Battalion remained in Billets at LES BALONS being gradually reduced to CADRE STRENGTH. On the 31st March, Two Officers and 100 Other Ranks (retainable personnel) were sent as a draft to the 1/5th Border Regt. Six Officers proceeded to join the 51st Manchester Regiment 2nd Army on the 27th March as volunteers for the Army of Occupation.	

H. Hollas. Lieut. Colonel.
Commanding 16th Service Bn Manchester Regiment.

16th BATTALION MANCHESTER REGIMENT.

WAR DIARY.
APRIL 1919.
VOLUME 42.

LES BALLONS.
HERSEAUX.
30.4.19.

W H Colley............Lieut-Col.
Commanding 16th Bn. Manchester Regiment.

Army Form C.2118.

WAR DIARY
or
INTELLIGENCE SUMMARY.
(Erase heading not required.)

Instructions regarding War Diaries and Intelligence Summaries are contained in F. S. Regs., Part II, and the Staff Manual respectively. Title pages will be prepared in manuscript.

Place	Date	Hour	Summary of Events and Information	Remarks and references to Appendices
Les Ballons.	1.4.19		The remaining personnel of the Battalion remained in Billets at les Ballons. Drafts of returnable Officers and men being posted to 3rd P.O.W.Coy. On April 30th the Battalion being down to CADRE strength awaiting orders for embarkation.	
Herseaux Belgium	30.4.19.			

W. H. Kelley .... LIEUT. COLONEL
Commanding 16th Service Bn. Manchester Regiment.

16 Manchester R.

96/2 4 3

WAR DIARY
or
INTELLIGENCE SUMMARY.
(Erase heading not required.)

Army Form C. 2118.

Instructions regarding War Diaries and Intelligence Summaries are contained in F. S. Regs., Part II. and the Staff Manual respectively. Title pages will be prepared in manuscript.

Place	Date	Hour	Summary of Events and Information	Remarks and references to Appendices
LES BALLONS. HERSEAUX. BELGIUM.	1.5.19. to 31.5.19.		The Cadre of the Battalion remained in Billets at LES BALLONS during the Month of MAY awaiting orders to proceed home. Orders for the reduction of Cadre strength to 3 Officers - 35 O.R's completed 9.5.19.	

W H Colley. Lieut.-Colonel.
Commanding 16th S. Bn. Manchester Regt.

Army Form C. 2118.

16 Manchester

WAR DIARY
or
INTELLIGENCE SUMMARY. W.H.C

(Erase heading not required.)

Instructions regarding War Diaries and Intelligence Summaries are contained in F. S. Regs., Part II. and the Staff Manual respectively. Title pages will be prepared in manuscript.

Place	Date	Hour	Summary of Events and Information	Remarks and references to Appendices
LES BALLONS	1/6/19 to 6/6/19		Cadre of the Battalion remained in Billets till 6/6/19. On 6/6/19 Cadre consisting of LT & Q.M. T.G. MILNER and 31 O.R. proceeded for disposal via LILLE Demobilization Camp taking Colours with them. W.H.C. LT. COL. W.H. COLLEY & 2/Lt McCAIN remained at HERSEAUX with Equipment Guard of 12 O.R. W.H.C.	
	3/6/19		Honours & Rewards Lt. Col. W.H. COLLEY awarded O.B.E (Military Division) Authority Gazette June 3rd 1919. W.H.C.	

W. H. Colley Lt Col
16th MANCHESTER REGT.

www.ingramcontent.com/pod-product-compliance
Lightning Source LLC
Chambersburg PA
CBHW081500160426
43193CB00013B/2549